More about Milky Way Accent...

Bob Snyder's poetry hitches the downhome to the sublime, the local—honky tonk, bebop, bus stations, and bedrooms in West Virginia and its global environs—to the galactic. Razor sharp, the poet's self-deprecatory wit, combined with this panoramic perspective, risks reducing all of us to the inconsequential. Instead, his egalitarian ridicule and awe make our small enterprises integral to the vastness of the Milky Way. With ideas filched from likely and unlikely sources, including comic books, opera, Medieval poetry, Beatniks, religious mystics, and Huey Long, his idiosyncratic warp drive carries readers from the playful dawn of "Aubade" near the beginning of the collection to the poignant concluding poem, "The Night Watch," with its well-wishing and omniscient sentinel.

—EDWINA PENDARVIS
writes about Appalachian life and literature. Her poems and essays have appeared in the *Appalachian Journal, Appalachian Heritage, Pine Mountain Sand & Gravel, Journal of Appalachian Studies,* and *Now & Then: The Appalachian Magazine.*

These poems are true - every one. True to the times, the places where we lived in those days. True to the voices, and true to love. Indeed, these are the finest love poems to my people and their way of being that I have ever known. Bob Snyder has given me back my own life here in West Virginia - the working class lives of my family and so many others who moved away to find work or be educated but kept coming back because they were of these hills and towns. Bob's rhythms, voices, and music get to the heart of us like no other writer of our time.

—JACK SPADARO
an Italian hillbilly from Mount Hope, W.Va.

MILKY WAY ACCENT

& Selected work

BOB SNYDER

DOS MADRES

2020

DOS MADRES PRESS INC.
P.O. Box 294, Loveland, Ohio 45140
www.dosmadres.com   editor@dosmadres.com

Dos Madres is dedicated to the belief that the small press is essential to the vitality of contemporary literature as a carrier of the new voice, as well as the older, sometimes forgotten voices of the past. And in an ever more virtual world, to the creation of fine books pleasing to the eye and hand.

Dos Madres is named in honor of Vera Murphy and Libbie Hughes, the "Dos Madres" whose contributions have made this press possible.

Dos Madres Press, Inc. is an Ohio Not For Profit Corporation and a 501 (c) (3) qualified public charity. Contributions are tax deductible.

Executive Editor: Robert J. Murphy

Illustration & Book Design: Elizabeth H. Murphy
www.illusionstudios.net

Typeset in Adobe Garamond Pro,
SF New Republic & Die Nasty

ISBN 978-1-948017-97-8
Library of Congress Control Number: 2020942596

First Edition
Published by Dos Madres Press, Inc.

Acknowledgements

MILKY WAY ACCENT

Appalachian Intelligencer,
Appalachian Journal,
Back Country,
Beyond Baroque,
Broccoli Seminar,
Cold Fire,
Dog Days,
Epoch,
Gone Soft,
Laurel Review,
Minnesota Review,
Mount Adams Review,
Night Season,
Phoebe,
Pigiron,
Pine Mountain Sand and Gravel,
Second Growth,
Soupbean Anthology,
Sow's Ear,
Strokes,
Unicorn,
Washington Review,
What's a Nice Hillbilly Like You... ?,
Wind.

SELECTED WORK

We'll See Who's A Peasant,
Mountain Union Books, 1977;

The Mason Dixon Sutra,
Igneus Press, 1999;

Old Martins, New Strings,
The Soupbean Press, 1990;

What's a Nice Hillbilly Like You... ?,
Antioch-Appalachia, 1976;

Old Wounds, New Words,
Jesse Stuart Foundation, 1994

Photographs

"Jack's", (Pittsburgh, PA) adapted
"Bus Stop", (Mason County, WV)
"Jesus", (Jackson County, WV)

Used by permission of West Virginia born poet and photographer GREG CLARY. Contact information: gclary@clarion.edu

"The Soupbean Poets"

BILL BLIZZARD, (1918–2009) Antioch Appalachia professor, West Virginia journalist

"Bob Snyder at Lees Junior College"

Used by permission of poet PAULETTA HANSEL, an original Soupbean Poet. https://paulettahansel.wordpress.com/

"Jimmie's, Beckley, WV 2020"

Used with the permission of the photographer, Stephanie Ketz

Gratitude

Without the help of West Virginia poet Kirk Judd this book would never have made it. Kirk was the guide who edited, encouraged and nudged. He was patient when others would have lost it. One can't say enough about how much he did to make this book a reality.

Thanks also go to another West Virginia poet, Edwina Pendarvis who was wonderful at editing. I feel like we worked smoothly and efficiently together. Pauletta Hansel, a Cincinnati poet, gave valued advice and recommendations.

Bob's widow, Peggy Snyder, owns the rights to Bob's work. She was generous and gave us the freedom and trust to put things together, offering only occasional comments. Her partner Charles D'Arville assisted with technical issues. Joan McCracken Barrett McAnany was a tireless cheerleader and inspiration to get Bob's last manuscript published. We are grateful to Bob's longtime friend Pete Laska who wrote the Preface to this book.

My first reader and critic is always my husband Sam Farley. To Donna Weisman, Barbara Freirson, Jack Spadaro, Amanda Farley, Luke Farley and all the people who have lent their emotional support, I owe many thanks.

These pages are owed to all of you!

—*Yvonne Snyder Farley*

To
Peggy,
Malwina,
and
Eff

Table of Contents

ЅELEϹTED POEMЅ

Foreword

Milky Way Accent mainly consists of the poetry manuscript left by my brother, Bob Snyder, when he died of a heart attack in 1995. Peggy Snyder, Bob's widow, asked me if I would move forward to have it published and gave me complete leeway as to how to get that done. Joe Barrett, the late West Virginia poet from Richwood and Bob's great friend, was published in 2018 by Dos Madres Press in a volume entitled *Blue Planet Memoirs* which Peggy and I really liked. We approached Dos Madres and the manuscript was accepted.

I took on this task because Bob was the greatest intellectual and artistic influence in my life as well as a playful and beloved older brother with whom I laughed so much and shared stories. He was very much a typical older brother who thought it was super hilarious the time that I got food poisoning and vomited all night long or that back when he was a lifeguard at the local swimming pool I attempted a dive off the high board and did a belly flop. On the other hand he had me reading Bertrand Russell when I was fourteen. I still miss him and think of things I wish I could talk with him about.

For several months I worked with poets Edwina Pendarvis and Kirk Judd to edit *Milky Way Accent*. Peggy asked Peter Laska to write the preface. Pete and Bob were intellectual companions over the years, working at the Antioch Appalachia Center in Beckley, WV, and, along with many others, publishing poetry together. The two were founders of a collective poetry group, *The Soupbean Poets*, who read throughout the region in the 1970s and connected with poets and writers all over Appalachia in a cooperative. It was a time when art and politics were blossoming in Appalachia.

Milky Way Accent contains poems selected by Bob but we felt that there were poems that we liked not included. Some poems from his first book *We'll See Who's a Peasant* were wonderful and thus came the section of selected poems. The poems in this volume as we have assembled them reflect love, family, West Virginia, crazy wisdom in the Buddhist tradition and countless other themes showing that in spite of (and because of) our hillbilly accents we are part of the Milky Way and the cosmos. "Follow the Tao" was his guide in poetry, life, music, politics and love.

His poetry was very much tied to his background as a native West Virginian who was born and reared in a small Ohio River Valley town of St. Marys. The legend is that this town was founded by the Virgin Mary who appeared in a vision to the founder. (Pete Laska once wrote "for reasons that were best known to herself"... She is mentioned in a poem.) Our parents were working class pro-union people and old FDR Democrats. My dad worked in the local Quaker State Oil Refinery and my mother worked as a clerk in the county health department. Bob was in High School before we ever owned a car. We lived in a rented house on Barkwill Street and walked everywhere. In those days the town was an isolated and intimate place where people were related and knew each other. During the Quaker State Oil Refinery Strike of the 1950s we ate food provided by the union's "jot 'em down store" and never forgot the names of the scabs.

My dad was artistic and did sign painting on the side. I remember him applying gold leaf on lettering he did on the local bank window as well as painting on canvases and spare walls. My mother always worked even before it became the thing for women to work. She taught piano and in retirement played keyboard in a band called the *Front Porch Swingers*. During World War II she worked in the local oil refinery and another time in the local marble factory. Both my grandmother Effa and my mother Malwina adored "Bobby" who was to some extent the little prince. Bob's sense of humor, which was legendary, came from my Dad and Mother.

With my parents both working, and during the World War II years, Bob was reared by my maternal grandparents, Fred and Effa Schmidt. Fred was a German-speaking glassworker and a follower of the American Socialist, Eugene Debs. As my mother grew up, the family traveled around to various glass factory towns. His family had been socialist and pacifist for as long as family stories can remember. The ethos passed on from Fred, as well as by my father's family, who had lived in Pleasants County for generations, was to study hard, learn, read, and be smart. Fred added class consciousness as a guidepost. My grandfather did have a pet crow and did make beer in his backyard during prohibition just like Bob's *Poem for my Grandfather* says. Later in life, Grandpa Schmidt worked at the state liquor store. A relative told me that my paternal great-grandfather Patterson was not known to work except on election day. He spent most of his time reading.

Much of Bob's poetry was influenced by our maternal grandmother's large family – the Cunninghams from Ireland, West Virginia. During the late 1940s most of the family migrated to Akron, Ohio, where my Great Aunt Ida's husband owned a gas station. There they congregated but kept the roads busy traveling back and forth to the hills of central West Virginia. It was a huge family and Bob's youth was spent traveling to country churches for funerals and reunions. They provided ample inspiration for a poet/writer.

The first poem I remember Bob writing was one that got him in trouble. As a boy he wrote a poem about three of his teachers in elementary school. "Triplett, Hammett and old Locke, all with solid heads of rock" are the lines I remember. Our family considered the poem the product of a child prodigy and was not seen as lack of respect. As a younger sibling I had to live down Bob's poetic efforts in elementary school. Having a big imagination, Bob left stacks and stacks of notebooks full of his illustrated adventure stories and poems from childhood.

Several of the poems in this book are about high school and people in St. Marys. Bob played football but had to drop out when he suffered a brain concussion. His nickname in High School was "Snake" and today on his tombstone in St. Marys his nickname is engraved. There are people still alive who call him Snake. Paine's Place was a beer joint on the hill above town (in another poem) where Bob logged many hours during his youth in St. Marys.

Thanks to a General Motors scholarship he graduated from West Virginia University in 1959 majoring in German and English and was Phi Beta Kappa. I think the only bad grade he received was in ROTC. By the time he left WVU he had become a Beatnik who remembered exactly where he was when Billie Holliday died. Many of the love poems are about a first love in Morgantown which I know didn't end well. He married Peggy Calkins who was a tolerant, intelligent and loving partner. The poem "*Aubade*" is dedicated to her.

With the help of Joe Samuels, Bob followed up with a master's degree in Philosophy from the University of Cincinnati. In Cincinnati he became a leader in the United

Appalachians of Cincinnati and was much influenced by an Appalachian organizer in the Over-the-Rhine area, Ernie Mynatt, and by Bluegrass musicians like Hank "Boatwhistle" McIntyre and his son Junior. Bob could play guitar and piano. A great tragedy for him was when his Martin guitar was stolen from his car during a bluegrass festival in Raleigh County, West Virginia.

In the early 1970s through a friend who was tied to the Antioch College Black Studies program, Bob initiated Antioch College/Appalachia in Huntington and then into the coalfields of southern West Virginia. He wrote in the school catalog that the Appalachian people "fit together in a "fabulous backbone way". There he used the prism of the Appalachian experience for undergraduate education. Students at the center came from Appalachia as did the teaching staff that included P.J. Laska, Don West, Bill Blizzard, Jr., Doug Chadwick, Everett Lilly, Ken Sullivan, Paul Nyden, Tom Woodruff, Rod Harless and myself.

It was at the Antioch Appalachia Center that the Soupbean Poets were brought together and published several books of poetry and short stories through Mountain Union Books, a press that they established. After the school in Beckley closed Bob entered Harvard and moved north. After completing his dissertation *"Cognition and the Life of Feeling in Susanne K. Langer"* he graduated with a Doctor of Education degree. His dissertation was dedicated "To Earl "Bud" Powell, in memory of one night of piano playing, at Basin Street East in New York City". The thesis of this work was "Susanne Langer constructed a rational framework for cognition and the life of feeling by inventing apt units through Gestalt spadework that fused science and philosophy." He called her a "musical metaphysician" who blended in rational unity these two modes.

Bob was someone people liked to party with into the wee hours of the morning as he played jazz and bluegrass records, quoted poetry, discoursed on philosophy, physics or whatever came up and left you the next morning with a hangover realizing that you had learned so much. He read widely and easily quoted from Basho, Catullus, Ginsberg, Sappho, or Villon. He told me once that if he had "it" (meaning intellectual pursuits) to do over again he would have learned learned Sanskrit first.

Everything was spiced with the spontaneous Crazy Wisdom of Buddhism.

His poetry managed to incorporate simple realities of life into the wider cosmic experiences and like others who appreciated his poetry I got it. Bob's poetry is based in places like Morgantown, St. Marys, Pennsboro, Richwood, Fenwick Mountain, the Quaker State Oil Refinery, Charleston's Summers Street, New York City and other locales that echo the greater human condition in their very commonness.

—Yvonne Snyder Farley
St. Albans, West Virginia
May 9, 2020 (Year of Quarantine)

Preface

When I met Bob Snyder in 1966 he was head of United Appalachians of Cincinnati, having been influenced by Ernie Mynatt, an activist from Kentucky. Bob had already published poems in small literary magazines, like the *Mt. Adams Review.* Near the end of the decade, he connected with Antioch College's expansion program and became Director of Antioch-Appalachia, first in Huntington, then in Beckley, a thriving city in the southern West Virginia coalfields in the Seventies.

With the Appalachian region as his educational lens, Bob fostered student poetry readings at the college, launched the literary quarterly *What's a Nice Hillbilly Like You...?*, published student poetry chapbooks, and supported the formation of the Soupbean Poets Collective, which in 1977 produced the Soupbean Anthology that became part of a burgeoning Appalachian literary renaissance. That same year he published his first collection of poems, *We'll See Who's a Peasant?* under the pen name Billy Greenhorn, which was not intended as a pseudonym so much as a literary persona of the youthful, innocent observer. It was then and still is a mystifying book. Leavened by humor and a playful zest for language, he subtitled it "poems of love and family." The poems about his family are placed first, with an epigraph from al Juwayni: *"Hold to the religion of the old women."* None of us at Antioch-Appalachia at the time had ever heard of al Juwayni, an eleventh-century Iranian philosopher and Islamic theologian, who wisely denied universal causality in favor of spontaneity (and miracles) in nature. The larger section of love poems documents the hazards of passion with inimitable poetic style. It has an epigraph from the fifteenth-century French poet Villon: *"Orde paillarde, dont viens tu?"* from his "Testament" assemblage recalling the women from his past. Bob was not a Villon-type poet (Villon died young, after a life of dissipation and brushes with the law), but he found common ground with Villon's wit, humor and admiration of women. Bob's admiration and sympathy for the plight of working class women in Appalachia is evident in the "Donna Jean" section of *Milky Way Accent*, which begins with her funeral. In "Dream of Donna Jean," the final poem in the sequence, we learn that her heart "stopped at twenty-two," her hand "naked of any wedding ring."

Bob was influenced by jazz greats and a variety of poets that included Japanese poets Basho, Issa, and Buson; Roman poets Lucretius and Catullus; the ancient Greek poetess Sappho, as well as Beat poets. He was friends with poet Joseph Barrett of Richwood, who introduced us to the Japanese satirical senryu form when the three of us gathered at the Baber Mountain Readings in the Eighties, where we agreed to collaborate on a book of poems as The Mason Dixon Trio. *Old Martins New Strings* was published in 1990, shortly before Joe's death. Nearly all Bob's poems in *Old Martins New Strings* are collected in *Milky Way Accent*, including the outstanding "The Night Watch," in which the poet identifies himself as "a satellite" keeping "an eye on the whole planet," from "lonesome cities lighting the Trans-Siberian Railway" to a friend's trailer "on Fenwick Mountain" in West Virginia, and says "I am ever so concerned about the Enlightened Democracies" and "the flames across the African grasslands/Amazonia dotted with slash and burn." Turning his eye to the campfire his friends have built, the watchman ends the poem with "a coal shining here another over there/what a spark-eyed sight to see."

In the early Nineties Bob and his wife Peggy were living in Boston. Bob was working toward a doctorate in education at Harvard, and was planning to write his dissertation on the philosophy of Susanne Langer. It was a triumphant time for capitalism and a low point for socialism. Harvard economists were in Moscow advising the KGB on how to become millionaire investors overnight. Bob agreed to accompany me to Gloucester, Massachusetts, to read with the Igneus Poets and Vincent Ferrini, the 80 year old "last Proletarian Poet," whose book, *A Tale of Psyche*, had just been published by Peter Kidd's Igneus Press. At Gloucester, and at Portland, Maine, and Boston's Piano Factory, Bob joined in the readings and closed with his poem "Grossvater," from *We'll See Who's a Peasant*. I remember the reception by audiences was electric. Amid shouts and whistles, he received standing ovations:

Poem To My Grandfather

My grandfather argued
With bugles of phlegm,
Said gurgle a gurgle a gurgle:
No one could win with him,
He was so full of whiskey
And the sweet juice of human meat.

He could gargle up a bubble
Of the cold wind whistling
On a poor man's knife:
He made wine out in the open

In the foreign part of town
Where the cops were scared to go.

Just before he had to quit drinking
Old grandad got a split-tongue crow
And he taught it socialism:
Wellsir, they used to sit up drinking in the kitchen,
The crow saying all men are brothers,
The old man gurgle gurgle, yes yes.

MILKY WAY ACCENT

Hold to the religion of the old women
—al-Juwayni

from *We'll See Who's A Peasant*

Birdtide

it was a day when thank God no musicians died
day when Pasadena said the rings of Neptune are complete
when Moscow told Warsaw to hey like cool it
it was a day when Bogota said it hoped
to extradite a major drug dealer to the U.S. and
the Lithuanians said annexation is void
day when Dreama said he's gone but'll be back a-Thursday
there dateline Miami with kingpins in her hair
where the caption said "trashy" and irresistible" funny
funny diction for the New York Times

yes it's a day when Dreama rambles on and on
in her hair-raising West Virginia accent
whah we don't do nothin wrong out hyar
just play yunno like brothern sister
day when she says Chuck won't tell where he went
why should he all a tham missin years
but he is tee totally off of the dope
hmmmmmm then what went down at the Baronesses
and plays reglar yunno down at Manny's Gringo Lounge
with young Chico on drums and some old colored guys
says sometimes I'll set in a-rappin in tongues
A KALLY MOE SHONDO (huh!)
ka dobba da freet wheel bee ooo wee

Aubade

if thieves come baby and steal the chairs
we wont get up   wont go nowheres
leave the cops and robbers to their own affairs
if thieves come baby and steal the chairs

ill push you down to China should your dream fly bad
so roll on up and kiss me and dont be sad
and think and just think of all the fun we had
to fall clear down to China when a dream goes bad

so wind flame diamond and the final fleece
down down dropping in the deep hearts peace
outside theyre nervous   theyre calling police
but wind flame diamond and the final fleece

OvaJean's Hot Flash

yes we know you've heard it all before
for we talk our loving in the mines
mine our coal all over in the bar
where you make cold eyes at our courting
toss your lurid locks and ignore us
pour Fuzzy Navel: Aztec Brakelight:
Mud Slide: Weeping Babylonian:
ring up "Rank Stranger" on the juke box

but opening the lonesome cooler
you sigh at capshine on the waters
whose healing chill first promoted you
booby first class to penguin easy
yes the warm red drunken racket dims
you're up in Christ's weary face again
and maybe it's time to call Mommy
go ahead it's your own cold quarter

Snake Snyder

my home county:
the last few dark farmhouses
whisper my high school name

All Hallows

burnt down the one candle
          blown out the tother
black burlap curtain pulled to orange moon
awake me from baked October dreams
too intact to name the white towel
you're stopping the broken pane chill with

I only half grasp your wink's warm circumspection
the room I was getting to know has swung southward
you this naked changeling lighting me a taper
hair mixmastered
          face spooky lemon
and I hearken to the Secret Word a-leaping
plumb down from the Starry Throne of Midnight
WHAT RECORD WOULD YOU LIKE TO HEAR
these autumn tunes grow each night wilder
the Thoroughfare of Heaven
          has changed its course

Shekinah

I take from out the storied drawer
the battered envelope with now brown glue
(how droll you would call me "Mr.")
brush the sparkles from the cool limp letter
it's all in the ballpoint of your hillbilly French:
"Notre ami, Runt, a quitte son travail
et il est maintenant a Clarksburg.
Pas ayant entendu dire de la recession..." from
that simple time and place
separated now naturally into simple facts
neither mixed up nor painfully confusing
concentric rings round the true original
these chromatographies of autumn
left behind by the solvent front

how unsupported by a single thought
all the mystical salts and crystals
leach out of old letter paper pores
into the larger life of September dawnin
emerald eyes a rag rug of welcome
softening the sun with Sothren care
top lip flattening with the feelings
beside me in your loose green paisley dress whose
folds so literal and allegorical
rustled so moral and mystical
that morn you drove me up and around
to the one-room schoolhouse where you taught round
the crackly bend so sweet of way
with its poppalorums high and low
to introduce me as your cousin

though even the slowest pupil knew different: "mais
de ce mot je ne connais rien-
savoir, comme dans le Bible..."

Vigil

the not yet loved let love tomorrow
tomorrow too the loved already—
look inside and see all silvery
the warm little sweet little scene
within the Chevy's haggard frame
en route the Apple rattling W.Va. tags
through thundering convoys of the Turnpike-
see your bare tired face beside me
mouth unpursed in slack z's of nod
hipness a mere furrow now twixt brows
your baby daughter dozing in back
with the Spring teddybear from the Fair-
it's no longer the Sex Heaven I supposed
egad no I'm a guard or godly driver
not really wanting out or wanting in
the car ahum a material harmony
and as the bluegrass gives way to bop
that lunar bug eye reads our funnies
it's printed right in to our pokey dots
we're bellringers riding up the ropes
me awake you asleep all one vigil
LISTEN WE MUST WORK OUT SOMETHING

Night Racket

I heard you pardon me the goofgonk
waking up your neighbors with empty garbagecans
clanging down the cement steps at four thirty in
    the morning
completely destroying the big oppressive brain
    glunk
of mutual love worry

I heard you laughing fit to be tied
behind your high dark windows way up
there on University Avenue
you knowing my character
                   me knowing yours

never before or since was
anything so pure or certain

Umbrella Theater

thought I heard the tinhat stovepipes say
we're stainy
          we're steamy
                  it's rainin' today
on dumb Morgantown shrouded in storm
and water meter covers in the alleys
on funny young us far from the curbs
us the twin totems of Grumbein's Island
blank and bug-eyed as fishin' decoys
marooned on the gem of the Traffic Isles
                  YESIREE
my Dixie Chicken Energy Hen ADAM
AND EVE WARNT NAKED
                WE ALONE ARE NAKED

the lover's excuse we began with
this dark afternoon has made its idol
all night we've reasoned
                brakelights redden our eyes
stand we pit pat empty as bug shells
stone droplets eating out of our hands
this place where murderers surrender
wet posturing raincoats
              keep our dead love alive
and I think I hear the Rain Maid say
they're windy
          they're rainy
              take them away

Adventures of Rainy Raincoats

on the night of knowing everything
vault lightnin brimmin blue Monday ridges
dark blocks flashin twelve thirteen windows
we shelter on the Westover Bridge
and at long last argue it to piece
naught but one sumpty bumpdom
naught but old self new
                          new self old
and I can taste the hoola moola
in the pelting hick town downpour
and you can touch the moola hoola
in the fluttery Greyhound ticket
them swart locks an rowdy heathen mess
finding but wet counsel in the storm
emerald eyes sinking the sun-boat
of dragon-apparent dream-concerns
as the bickybye streetlights beckon
and the *chic*ly stiffening raincoat
tells my chilled-out fingertips we've
cracked heads deep in some pyramid
true to West Virginia in our fashion
O the umbrella funerals of Nefertiti
on the night of knowing everything

M-Town Freezies

radiant storm has crossed the Blue Ridge
sweeps yes the long Willey Street curve
where staring from the doorway of a shop
the depressed priest inhales a menthol
for thar ye blow my nervous Ninevite
your Maybellene vial of Chicago green
clinking against the pint of bourbon
deep in that rainy raincoat pocket

dozened in macintosh arroyos
the blue ballpoint Baudelaire awash
chic beltknot thrown in a God forbid
bareheaded   collar up   pallorous
earrings so bare so extra seeming
stray black hairs coiled like shavings
in the hour of wanting everything
stride by in Messallina sneakers

drops flown up from Rio smite your cheek
no won't let you doubt being buried
but a sleepy dreamsteep hour ago
in the musty Andes of your quilt
dark monks stalking and billygoats gruff
step by heartbeat step crost Grumbein's Island
none dare break your whitened roughened spell
lest you lose track of hoarflash clovers

blacker whiter than heart's dim grey lore
M-town's everlasting urge to leave
catches you by the shivering heels
for one last swing down the Casbah
to these rainstiles' tunnelsome end
where your lame duck paces linoleum
where you'll smile and count down his spines
your leaving-love thirstier than rain

Mexican Standoff

there's a mip mop of thunder
when I defend my old school ties
that dumps the dark insides out
lets loose the white wha hunh
and hm it's Morgantown West Virginia
Start: Beginning: the Kiss Continuous
because there's no Substitute for Anything
it streaks down to the sidewalks
from Woodburn Hall's gingerbread rooves
and away out on the Monongehela
chickie in a dad gum bread pan
it bops itself silly in void barges
and atop our dreamsteep M-town hill
on the blind grey porch of your pad
it sashays through the babywire
hoarily filling with wet born green
as we sit smoking in the doorway
our romantic hassles insoluble
just hailing the leeways of life

To Blossom Dearie

O the women of the fifties
hard-loving women of the fifties
the slinky smoke of their cigarettes
rides in rings to the everlasting
ebb and flow of human music—
for one reefer lights another.
In raincoats and sneakers they greet me
HI BOBSVILLE WHAT'S HAPPENING
to a Lestorian "Just Friends"
with stories of exes and lovers
in jealous little pictures, off,
a private collection of worries
come down from *La Boheme.*
Out of love and boppawhatnot
they made me their historian
showed me what to feel and when
and how to slide with the seasons
(going through changes, doing takes)
                              all that
I owe to the women of the fifities

The Genius of Apple Daddy's

—To Bobby Garland

bet she had the Beckley cops turning cartwheels Bobby
after she shot you your fatal yes fatal girlawhom the
Legal Law set scot free
but I knew you big town and small
the main man of Swann Street in D.C.
chief troublemaker of Beckley West Virginia
throwing shoes squawking like a chicken in the Fayva
mooning the dinner for Congressman Nicky Joe Rayhall
because you knew Marx you knew Malcolm X
knew your *Egyptian Secrets of Albertus Magnus* cooling it
there with your schoolmarm mom
seeing into the bloodshot heart of things

driving north Bobby a hundred miles from your grave know
at the very moment you passed I knew
lipped through my window in telepathic dream
know you come back now in midsummer voodoo
as I recall driving your mom and you to the Hill
when you spot Fish and Sedena and yell get in
and the Missus says "Bobby, you needn't shout so loud!"
and you wide-eyed and sweating from the pills
her little boy smiling then like Albertus Magnus
streetishly you yell "They Tack Heads, Momma!
Momma! You got to talk loud to Tack Heads!"

Beatnik Perfume

this mirror of chill silver
seems more to you like
a dognosed snowflake or like
what remains when mind has melted
burned bathroom walls utterly away
dissolved the whole funky building
skeletons and treasure maps and hidden drugs
the hill it is on and all of M-town
the earth even and the solar system
and the hickiest reaches of the kosmos
only the ice-cold exciting Void abiding
only the this freckled medicine chest mirror
where your every morning face
sniffs the stale talcum gleam
puzzled by thoughts of mercy
bewildered by the idea of fair play
yes yes the pure version of romance
is like asking for justice in a clip joint:
where you stare at yourself
practicing up how to fool me
going from perception to thought
from thought straight to perception:
where bugged by hail-colored verticals
by corny laurel springs at the top
you yank open the BOING-dy door
and irritated by the rusty razorblade slot
yet once more by the caked toothbrush holder
you reach past the Q-tips and baby aspirin
past the benzedrine and amyl nitrate
pat the atomic holocaust suicide pills
to your one pitiful bottle of beatnik perfume
                              mind made up

Recursion

dreamt I met you in New York City
Forty-Eighth Street off of Eighth Avenue
ticket for home sighing in my pocket
you too drunk to tell lies—

I seize you by the clothy arm
and try to tell you how momentous
but you're limber as wind chimes
ripped and Egyptian like an ostrich—

I try to give you the book about us
but you guard your big black beatnik purse
peculiar over it the way you were
over that Cincinnati wedding band—

and now you're laughing saying
hey why are there always treasure maps of
infinite temptation
                    like to my stash in M-town
in the little dwarf door in the kitchen baseboard—

and suddenly we're in the Time Square subway station
and I've lost you in a crowd of Hawaiian Wormheads

Kerouac in Charleston

humble illusory self
                 walk honorable streets
though Neal is restless
                 doesn't dig hillbilly music
Jack's home in the Keltic Kingdom
like Charlie Chan in China

the junkie's tires screech
                 the tard gapes
rows of red paper bells
                 light up a chill sunset
and Ti-Jean strides south on Summers Street
toward the Boulevard and the Kanawha River
seeking what-to-do with his unreal ego
on the half hour layover in Charleston
half-crummy   half-distinguished
his raging Keltic eyes draw to Spyro's Lounge
his alligator shoes drawn toward the river
his sperm climbing upstream toward the country gal
in a silk Kyoto jacket and navy ring

unknown to Jack she's choongum thinking
Lordy me I hope Judge Knapp
    don't put Dukey in jail
    and Jack picks up on the blind vibes of it
livens to Chinatown horror of sad West Virginia night
and when the silverward hits the floor
piing   plang   plong   plung
sunfaced Mason says to moonfaced Dixon

we got to draw no line nowhere

Chicken City

the old fart
sits on the porch
Mayor of Chicken City

Billy Greenhorn's Tradegy

let me go you dirty dog
it's Billy Greenhorn I love
(sez Heloise to Abelard)

and Mark Anthony smooches Cleopatra
right dead on top of a yawn
yes yes she rolls them Egyptian eyes
and sighs   and says
O to have been born in the future
in the province of West Virginia
then I could have obtained a REAL MAN

and there he sits at midnight
on the cold cold statehouse steps
nestled on the Orion Bridge
two thirds out the Milky Way radius
cheated out of the governorship

hats off   hats off
to the Great Beer Joint Poet

Welfare Witch

Buster the canary mummed an oh
No sooner than your slick sole hit sill.
Goldfish huddled behind the white chateau.

Poor Granny was all refrigeration:
Her scrupulous blue hair was faradized,
So hair-raising ran your reputation.

You were tickled. This gal's famous, I thought.
You tossed creek gypsy hair, flashed green eyes.
Trashy.   Irresistible.   Hot to trot.

And gave out such a wild will to show
What went past sireening. Here was
Stronger scythe. Broader swath. And longer row.

West Virginia's Darlin' Gal

you're no more'n inside the roadhouse door
when everyone winks and whispers your name
and law! you're not one bit embarassed
but just tickled that someone—someone!—cares

the men look at you and think
                              IT PARTY TIME!
the women look at you and think-
                              O never mind!
it's the manifold makes the appearance

for you the pay phone rings off the hook
for you bats circle Butch's shingle job
on the roof of the roistering honky-tonk
for you Roy lurks in the parking lot
nursing a tire iron for his rivals
for you they load up Wing Dings in Moorefield
for you the politicians steal the gold foil
plumb off the capitol dome
                              and for you just you
the lil orphans in red sweatpea pajamas
fold their sleepweak palms and pray for sugar

Comfort Me with Hyssop

in soft pencil my great grandmother Caroline
underlined all the most pessimistic parts
of her cheap littleprint 1880s Bible—
how like a flower we spring up in the morning
are cut down by evening: no wonder,

what with Lloyd's lifelong whiskey habits,
Eva her youngest dreadfully burned to death
while stirring that kettle of family clothes,
not to mention the vast screendoor boredom
of dingly back country cattle farming.

Wonder at her finding the inside outside
in the giant void growing on Mill Creek.
Wonder her way in the quiet mineral grass,
how many keys there are to heaven's rooms
but a broken heart's the axe to every door.

Merle

the whole outfit under grass:
I can't believe it! why
they were the whole slow life of me
and I was the kid at every funeral
Guy's with the four old farmers singing
their billygoat song up in the hills
Hughie's when I saw with a chill
that just like Uncle I too must die
Neilly's the baby of the family
that one really tore up her sisters

but I knew the hour had come
when at Lena's service up in Akron
my father stood blankly in front of Hughie's widow
"why my Lord Merle I didn't recognize you..."
Merle unrecognized by the eye of man!
Merle the prize by marriage
Merle Cotton and Buddy's mother
the family beauty a big sound forceful blonde
whose name people liked to say Merle Merle Merle
who always stood intent arms folded leant forwards
as if she were patiently enduring the cold
and you sort of want to offer to
run and get the poor woman a sweater
but no no Merle says
                and it's your move pilgrim
Merle looking you dead square in the eye
and you can't tell if Merle'll speak or laugh
for both start the exact same frank way

Family Dreams

truck traffic the one outside sound
our teevee's a pure silver fizz brimming out
the seas of fine deeds
the Old Man's asleep in the La-Zee-Boy stretched
out full of Falls City
drunk   slackjawed   dead to the world but in
that slumber suddenly
cocking his slouch hat back
beaming
never missing the chance to be a hero

Grandma

stiff as a weed in winter
with a fading goldengold clasp
the purse Mother kept of yours
so like the one which yielded
all kinds of funny book money
up here in the dreamsteep attic
opening it up reaching in
and from your very last pack
smoking one of your Phillip Morrises
separating my life into childhood and age
the blue brown smoke doing my heart good

Donna Jean

When you were my second bus heart-throb,
high solemn in pigtails and brogans,
I shoved your swing 'thout knowing why;
but as the puppy days spent down
growth stirred in a doubtful viewpoint,
a teen phase and a teen promise—
the blind foreground now just lifting.

And you'd have seasoned out I'm sure
from what all our dumb feelings said,
hidden in the cruel roles of the stages.
But who could have ever supposed
that it would all come down to this:
soft words on your twenty-one-odd years
over a cold funeral home cup of coffee.

Classmates

out of the foghorn walnuts
where crows loaf the cliffs
you eased your rustling kite
into the spark-eating lightning
finding a bleached bright easement
above the whitecapped Ohio River
so young to die   well I swan
let pass this unknown reality of our era
sleep in your Magic Minnie cloud forever

and let these motes in the sunbeam
so selfless firm and fully packed
still hypnotize the childish philosopher
who's never seen golden atoms before
only funerals
                    solemn country funerals

Donna Jean's Original Face

I see why you took such a grim picture:
You'd mess up a grin, ball up your fists like
You wanted to jump on the photographer
For making boys what they are, high school so.
"Giggles", we called you. You were easy amused,
Stopped helplessly there in hallways, trembling,
Scoops of snickering brimmed in your hand.

But on second thought, that gym assembly
With four hundred-odd Blue Devils that day
In the afternoon orange indoor light,
The girls screaming and stomping, the boys
Looking at legs, looking at each other,
Rolling their eyes at the female basketball.

Your shirt-tail hangs straight down.
                   What's to stop it?
Your blouse-front is raised but slightly
Like a dishtowel over two last biscuits,
But you stare so earnestly at the basket,
Cornfield arms akimbo, calm for a change,
Itching your tanny shank with your sneaker.

The Big Bang keeps on juggling itself
Like a volcano full of smogobogoes:
Left started: keeping started by itself:
Yes, the Big Bang keeps on juggling itself
And, land's sakes, ain't so awkward after all Stealing a
couple steps on a town coquette
With a move finer than film or photo,

Often read about but seldom seen,
Taking that bambino to the hoop
With a soft guttural burst of action,
With a wonderful drawling rookie deed!

Yes, blink and a hick town is past!
But a javey huntress is half a blink faster
When she kicks back a lean hind leg
Quickern you can eat a daggone prune
And lets fly her Raven Rock jump shot
So Momma-down-low, so simply deluxe!
And what it is possesses her to giggle
Is what possesses her to put on sneakers
At the sound of the buzzer: is what possesses
All us bodacious hillbilly niggers
So eager-ready at what we hope for.

The End of All Preludes

be freed of mirroring mind
stop the ant-wars of sentient thought
was defined in the contours of your outline
almost but not quite a nervous wreck
that hair's breadth sublimation of horror
trembling firmly always atop your troubles
like the live model for the Quaint Old Maid
perhaps when she was very very young
learning to withstand or conquer suffering that
facecard which Mother and Grandma used to
take such delight in dealing me shaking with
such female hilarity

yes   be sure
in the coming better comical dawn
your benday face will repeat itself
page upon page
                        saying underneath
in its Sunday best calligraphy
HERE IS THE STRONG NEW COUNTRY GODDESS

Pilgrim Number One

What a pale and crazy face made you then
from your high-up foggy schoolbus winder
on those raw restless chilly schoolmorns,
sky heavy-shrouded, whose webby darkness
leaked into every room, every heart,
the waking body itself sick of living
in the hazy orange light of gloom
of the painful graded school corridors-
though the one thing definite and clear
was your long and level grin
even with your lip bit white below.
And not till years later would we fathom
the secret of your girlish eagerness,
how your mother's female fears,
your father's chasing you with butcherknives,
put you up in the foreground of yourself
with pure politeness of that mouth and eyes laughing, saying,
"NO MORE TROUBLE PLEASE!"

Dream of Donna Jean

Secretly, you made light of all mouths, your
clever fingers poking politely
at snaggle canines and stupid molars:
and those whose teeth you ground on
never guessed what circus touched them.

Sometimes I dream of driving to Marietta,
straight to the office where you worked,
and you buff each tooth plumb sparkling,
buzz my gums good-naturedly once or twice,
give my big novocaine nose a peart shove:
your hands taste cinnamon and alcohol,
medical bitters and country clay,
all the mystical salts and crystals,
naked of any wedding ring and without
whatever would be the taste of death.

You swore you'd never marry, but
you asked after me to my mother every
time you ran into her up street.
That makes me ponder and worry:
did your thought of life move your way after
you left out from West Virginia?

Your heart stopped at twenty-two,
a naughty mousetrap click in the night.
Only later was I told how you let
the gym girls feel your pounding chest,
the history of dying young in your family.

After high school we met but seldom.
Lordy, didn't you look good that snowy evening
by Ogdin's Five and Ten on Main Street,
grinning like a monkey in a war bonnet,
your overswirl of hair right at long last,
with your heartbreaking small town perfume.
And I can't resist the brute judgment
that in the coming American Dream
it's your face we will kneel to and worship.

View from the Catwalks

Some days it's a happy balance of steam
as if every last cloud were our refining
other times a sorry hoohaw and a stench
too cruel a sweetening for any nose
but when that girl clutches the stormwire
with the silvery lunchpail for Pap
hell is harrowed for one little span
at what her young eye might be scaling
what a faraway tune her lips be poised on

A balm grows in the Foster-Wheeler
in the octane unit and the Dubbs Still
and even though it's not the Whistle
no no nor even the Five Till Five
there's a yeddyfwy above the Wax-House
when she raises the bail of the morning
and gawks into the pipefitter's nightmare
eyes a doe's frozen in sudden jacklight

Down the Orchard Hill has she come
past the fiery mane of the Burn Pipe
into screeching menace of explosion
to pass it through the Train-Gate
and sniff the crude cracking in the air:
when she shouts CAN I GO TO THE PARTY
and he hollers back through the fence NO
we know not now but in a minute
big hot tears knock grasshoppers down

Mysterious High School

People run up to me asking about the athletics of Mysterious High School and I say:

Hoo, haw.

Hath not Mysterious High burst open every game of every name in the Mid-Obscurity Conference, breaking every record every moment of every contest?

The formation of the football team is the backfield at the top of the mountain and the line at the bottom of the sea.

Lo, after the game, in the enemy dressing room, they weep to highest heights and deepest depths.

The baseball team dances and yodels in the field, creating fright with the fear of goo-goo.

At bat they think of the strike zone only when freedom is the athlete of detail, only when the baseball sleeps in the bellows of the swing.

And their basketball team—what an outfit!—their basketball team simply stands around smoking and looking at an iron basketball bolted to the concrete.

They have learned to dribble on the tips of their minds.

Hurrah for the Momeraths of Mysterious High School!

Their credits are worthless everywhere!

And patience.

Believe in Mysterious High School: lay your money on their coming season:

And watch for their school sweater: it is a swarm of funny-looking little black letters on a field of

Up State

brimstone slagtown time-out skies
where the Virgin umpires your life
chalk eggs pile up on the scoreboard
in front of the damp dapper scarecrow
waiting and waiting for the moon to complete

where new forms of dishwashing
are invented then clean forgotten

where the strikes steal porkchops
leave bulldog gravy powdered milk

where the plumbing makes yodels
all through the live long nights

where yellow daisy-eyes flutter in millsmoke

where she shakes her hair down: grins

Fairing Up

In the stormwashed rain barrel
Wiggletails
Surround the new fallen plum.

MoogaBooga Bible

God twocritter frog em i-stop long Baibel,
Twocritter frog long Baibel.
Wonem fashion twofella em i-stop long discritter buk?
Alltime em i-stop long discritter buk alltime alltime.
Alltime twocritter goodcritter alltime alltime.
Onetime God i-tok: "Meyou pusspuss, Froggie."
Onetime Frog i-tok: "Meyou pusspuss, Goddie."
Singsing twocritter em i-ketchum plenty singsing.
God twocritter frog em i-puttum allsame othercritter shirt,
Em i-gamblum long card,
Em alltime twocritter goodcritter.
Wonem twocritter em i-eatum?
Toodark pie long kaballah allberry.
Rain i-kom, now twocritter em i-hideum long Buk belong
    Revelations;
Sun i-kom-em-up-em, now twocritter em makum nabeach
    towel long Buk belong Genesis.
Em i-toodark, now em i-gamblum gen more long card:
"Seven belong toad!"
"Numberone bigfella belong trapezoid!"
"Jack belong fig!"
"Ace belong myrrh!"
Twocritter em i-tok: "Gen wecritter pilum gen!"
God i-tok: "Goodcritter!"
Frog i-tok: "Singsing!"
Goodcritter! Singsing! Alltime alltime!

Telescope Whiskey

What ran me to the Slinky Moon
is exactly what runs me from it:
Beerjoint's roistering dimmed to wind,
beer left tasting vinegar and sand,
driving from
        so lightly like
                driving to
it roughs up the shadows of repeating—

I pull off on that orphan asphalt
dead-ending in crumbling white posts
left sliced from *old* Old Route Fifty-
Dead-set my bottle on the warm hood,
forming that storied form serene
all in the shape of catering manna-
Swallow like some old telegrapher
on the far western borders of Love
full of arrows getting off one last dit-
Gawk straight up autumn's ghost beeches
at squirrel nests in the Milky Way
where the dark wells blither in hellglow
like a campfire kicked into mean streaks—

Constellated darkness says one thing
the Via Lactea quite another—
I was the fond notch in your lovelight
leaning above your coarse green irises
with their close-packed GROW UP SAILOR spokes
round the wee dot's black funnel to glee—

Night skies marquee our karmarama
  me lost in the stars
                and you
    pitched out of hell
              for playin in the ashes

Bob's Bodacious Flashbacks

it comes to me when I've been too long in the bar
musing over Rolling Rock in the back booth
and Sitting Bull winks down from the picture of Custer's
  Last Stand
and says hey Bob I really like your nine-syllable jump
  style meter
as do the rest of my murderous braves
ain't that right, Running Wolf?

it comes to me in great peopled stadia
in the spinetingling roar of the mob
that your ratty old love was perfect
in the rain delay paltering the lime
that we used our overblown crania
for no other goal than showing off

it comes to me in flick a flick fireworks
dit dark ballgame brief excuse-me-mams
brightly verging matron maid or hag
into the almost not quite face of you
here! but no
        there! but no
              FADEROO

and it comes to me a long drawn out Chinese opera
when the singers' heads commence to look orange
to say how politely we courted our year away
when the singing all sounds like "Red River Valley"
YEE GA DOO
      YEE GA DEE

YEE GA DOO DOO

to say thank you thank you
                        your kisses were outstanding

Maya Maya

a man ought to be able to say
when he likes a woman's brogue
it's like standing in a high high meadow
in the middle of an endless afternoon
watching the clouds make fools of themselves

but the imagined dialogue of feeling
drawn through the varying degrees of dignity
    of soul
immeasurable in its candid bliss
oh boy
what a disaster in reality

and thus it was that when I
dropped everything to go and see you
drunk in taxis   drunk in planes
on a rising curve of fantastic hope
your dismal eyes held not a thing
after me saying: have a good trip
after you replying: impossible

Patchwork Passion

to play on this quilt
would take oh
fifty different kindsa checkers

Mons Veneris

trying to cool it alone with a baby
makes of your life such goof hermitage nothing
to be seen but men men men
melting away the *haute franchise*

once in a rare while slips through an Orval
there's a rent in the Big Bead Curtain
and it's yet another sexual payday
(surely surely someone will rue the night) "Men!"
you hiss pronouncing your karma
but some way far off your heart is changed
and you breathe out smoke
                            leave off the gas
find rest at the steep uphill intersection
where the red light's stuck and you don't mind
where the elms all meet above
             and your mother will never find you

Ashes

the crunch of cinders makes
a clean break with the world
for suddenly I am raised
like a can-can grasshopper
far far into the substance of the charm
the infinitely glamorized neuralgia
of the roses' aching hour
                    hush red moon
on my wonderful windbreaker
I knock with edgely logic on the sandpaper
of your three room backdoor apartment
with thought thoughtful intensity
while moonlight rattles your windows
and the wind fondles those stiffy weeds
whose name in death even you alone would know

Odi Et Amo

You'd meant to be kind:
that really terrifies me.
Why, as it was, even,
the way you done me
would have made Hitler brush off his armband
with a shitty little grin.

You seemed so nice
stovetop burner whispering hoarse
rain B.B. traying on the window
of your three-room stagecoach apartment
when you would tell me
your story long and droll
smoking cigarettes drinking beer
fixing a late-night love-breakfast
HULA HULA GOES THE BACON

Seemed so damn nice. Yes,
that's why I wanted to
beat you to death
O you wild child pilgrim
with a piece of your iron-legged kitchen furniture!

Marvellous Circumspection

why you put your bread in your icebox I'II
never understand till the day I die
why it gave it a Tunisian smell
and standing there staring at the tall Rhine
  wine skyscraper
brain lit up like Saturday night in glittering
 Yokahama
itchy tomboy no got dough to meet ya
I hear you come into the kitchen
from the dark surprising bedroom
grinning like a hyenareena

pronouncing my name with marvellous circumspection

Recuerdo

This mornin we came back, hand in hand,
home from our innocent flight.
Mortal as moonshiners.   Living targets.
The entirety of our mortal luck
        half-piled in one brain,
                half-piled in the other.
Bickering on the pull-off gravels
took us through the undoctored night.
Radio Pittsburgh under the stars
where Mason and Dixon drew the line.
We clung to every lovesick utility.
Staked our fate on smoking home fries.
Breakfast at Mom's Place,
        corny over-tipping
                mumbles us dreamily home.
Back again, yes back again. And hey! outside this
        floating bedroom
                where could we be?

New York Woman

The passionate rain of the city
Sucks upon your window
Like the spattered bird of paradise
On the windshield of a carnival truck
In West Union, West Virginia:

That single New York hailstone
Is the snarling pearl
In the hot grey water
Of your mother's of a Monday Maytag
(Shake your money maker):

That green lightning gleam
Is the smash of lightning bugs
Under the nodding wipers
Of the luminous carnation buggy
That drives your sothren laughter
Over your poor old faded daddy
Standin cryin in the rain.

Billy Greenhorn's Mortuary Fan

when I told her my dreams
the shadows of my hands moved faster than my hands
I told her that
and she said "Robertito,
you are completely mournful,

you, you pale little mourner,
here—let me straighten your bouquet,
you, who've never been in love before"
(that's what 'twas)
tell her this is hers
tell her her illusions' secrets
("my illusions' secrets!")
her her dreams

Bahwnb

when you spoke my name
I was summoned wholly—
I was you, I was me...

Billy Greenhorn's Scavanger Hunt

should you ever find the letter
with her chilly day cottage
I'm the guy in the derby
at the horizon line of the *Great Books*
peeking over Ptolemy and Plato
as she kicks off earth's clay tablets

seablown head from the *Birth of Venus*
that's her atop the spring fashions
beige blouse pendant and moccasins
posies posies running round her slacks
as she capers off *The World of Mathematics*
commanding Yin and Yang's coy spotlight
hands folded behind her—uh—waist

hers the tilted sailboat script
that quotes I've a nice tree
from her father's holiday call
tells herself must stop saying daddy
then breaks into a fruitcake drawing
fish-leaves flying in dots to pockets
ladybug earrings and fractal mobiles
symmetrical cats inside glass frames
one strung to a shyly drawn penis

and if you've gone that far in it
read past the last passionate mantra
with its love you miss you respect you
worship you dragsville here we are
and behold the awkward sneaken bow

of the low-sketched critter whose features
are inscribed on an orange duck bill
cut no doubt from the same roto pages
as Aphrodite of the *Parkersburg News*
that Sunday in sleepy old Greenwood
and bring me please a leaf from the sea
to feed that hungry duck beak being

Aere Perennius

though always more or less of a Robin Hood to women
"lambey pie" was just a spark in the sky
the day you bought a pack of marshmallows
lit up for yourself a bonfire of my letters
held them powdered jokers to the flames of
McCrory's stationery and Scripto by-spice
blew glowy ashes from the bumparoos
                              so mouth-watering hot

                    and every since
it shakes with ashes from the secret fire
feathersome glints hop out of the Imperishable
and it dawns on me what an S.O.S. of devilment
your five-and-dimer of a Dear John message is
tapped out by the old arrow-filled telegrapher
                              yet and still
I'm circled by red stars from the pyramid
where we two graverobbers cracked heads in the dark
outward yes outward the waves from the drowning hair
and thank you   thank you   thank you
                              your kisses were outstanding

Goof Supreme

Love is bold anticipation, mostly:
that hitch in your step
them green omens in your eyes
when you ran up to me
brushing past poor old Lonnie
in front of the Gore Hotel in Clarksburg
me vacating all mental reflexes
forgetting all my wisecracks
squeezing the tear-water out of you

planning then to be with you forever.

Morning on Donnally Street

I found myself in the wholesale district wandering
past the warehouses printshops stormwired
pavinglots blank fishy offices
and storefronts of little jobbers busy inside
the streets and walks lonely as long bridges when
down the middle of the road comes
the Wholesale of the Wholesales
in her fuzzy tangerine bedroom slippers
bright red Afro comb
        clutched in her skinny fingers her
eyes upturned to God in Heaven
the way you do when something's in 'em
her exasperated bass voice hollering
over and over   again and again
KISS MY BLACK ASS
            YOU OVERSEEIN' MOTHERFUCKER

Lonesome Kosmosis

of all my island universes
               you most island lagoon
ringed with hoko moko berries
inland those moko hoko stone gods
and your ever-threatening uh oh volcano
                    YIKES SAKES
you have nothing to do with anything

in the dark deeps that never join
in that cold country back bedroom
shrunk-voiced   pale-faced kissing
me in dead earnest why
say it   say it   you said
and after wondering what 'it' was
and saying the wrong thing twice
castaway then on your beach
in the boogie woogie solitude where
the tide goes hula hula
ulp said it said ulp I love you

Aquarian Dread

to have me in your wetsome clutches holding
hands in the fish museum
where giant tuna snap at bubbles
circling gliding the big tank around
and in the small tank lined Disneystore
the glass shrimp show off their innards nary a
whet embarrassed at all

no jailhouse fish more antsy than I from
dowsing for the open water
my God do I want to escape you yet one
more natural enemy
you freckled Heebie-Jeebie Woman you scaring
the minnies with your giant face
when you smile into the lit lil habitats
while predation gathers in your eyes
like demented emerald hunger
"Ooh, look at this one, Bobby Boy!
Come back here and see what I see!"

An X-Man's Xes

the day Fat Jack Eagle entered nirvana we made
love in a country churchyard
Miss Sunbeam winked from her billboard
it rained cats and dogs the whole way home

the evenin' Fat Jack Eagle entered nirvana
the road from Saint Marys to Sistersville
was no where near as long as the way back *purusha*
and prakriti were distinguishable
in the soot that fell from the B and O train

the night Fat Jack Eagle entered nirvana
the candle burned right down into the carpet
the chianti flowed like blood Mississippi
dawn came up on partiers in sleeping piles

the mornin' Fat Jack Eagle entered nirvana
he woke up way before anyone else did
from a dream of swordfighting with Columbus
put on his corny underwear in the dark
and left before anyone knew he was gone

Doppelganger

The two-headed goat
butts and butts
the rain-soaked scarecrow.

Cartwheels and Millstones

like slow-boiling clouds on the mountain
your lips stir as if to tell me sumpin
but bright idea outshines speech
as a witch despises water
and shyful of the plan
                and hidden hey sure like
the county line in cloudburst
your mind to wander shows out only
in the emerald millstones of your eyes

fine fine wings just a-sproutin' out
from my bliss ninny back blades
I stand there jealous of Mexico
the focus of your playful wish
hey sure we could spill boozeworms
in the cantinas of Oaxaca uh Mother
end up at Carnaval in old Rio
bared in parley by the barest thirst

yes Love I know you hushly well
like a long long rainy car ride
purple riffles in flashbulb lightnin
Dairy Queens in white-tile Exxons
as we wend our fool romantic way
up Greenwood Hill past that shed
home of a hundred shaky businesses
each one a—blap!—hillbilly success

Joshu's Pet Shop

I saw your name written in truck dust
dug your face on a big denomination bill then
what seemed to be you yourself passing me in
a black Chevy
but when the distinctions dissolve into
that which is similar to itself
and not dissimilar to any other
why I'm sailing the Good Ship Amnesia
through seastorms of your Hollywood bed
my glow wicky socks hung on your lamp
your K-Mart ear rings in my wine glass
Buddha's sox all mixed up with my sox
today's sox tomorrow
                tomorrow's sox today
"Joshu's Pet Shop!
              Joshu speaking!"

Jijimuge

only in recognition of pure doom
does October stop here perfect
dark green many of the apple trees leaf-
schooner in the horse-bucket parched
bricks of the concave lane
broken off intact just when and where your
lover's heart reaches just ready
to embrace the world's each and every
equiprimordially with its Lambey Pie

only in the formkabob of Buddhahood
does October sit down under the tree
swearing not to budge till satisfied
strong step whole again from the shadow back
from Jataka-tales of past lives schnockered by
change's stately cider
and I am that white elephant
you are that great cunning hunter you
oldtime mystery woman you

Killtime Blues

a slow Monday:
the voice of the loudmouth
penetrates the beer cooler

Spring in Glen Jean

so when his buddies brought
his lonely lunchbucket home
she looked plumb through
those empty streetclothes
sitting there numb with fumbling
burnt the corners of her twisted hanky
with a Chesterfield cigarette
making her own dogwood legend

Confusion in Columbus

I slink into the Columbus bus station
                              escaping
cause she dear-Johned me in my gorilla suit
and there sits yet another madwoman
                              muttering
"nary one of them went over to the hospital...
over there with toenails like ram's horns..."
and the red-haired old lady looking for her friend
                              yelling
"Beebie! Beebie! You know better than that!"
and everyone turning wondering hey what's this
turns back to eat their scrambled eggs not knowing
and I board the throbbing Greyhouse for West Virginia
after the black newly weds who mount waving
                              smiling
as their people pingle the rice to our bus

Agony in Akron

it was so so simple
to buy you your ticket
to carry for you your little suitcase
    but it was agony in Akron

no trouble whatsohoohoo ever
exchanging spendthrift conversation
as the minutes spilled off
    but it was agony in Akron

and without a trace of bother
to hear your immortal farewell
"maybe I can sit next to a sailor"
                  FUN
in Morgantown West Virginia
    but agony in Akron

Night

high hill or clouded moon?
as I walk the hollow's darkness
with freezing feet
thinking
they are fixing to tear down
every house we ever made love in
(good thing we done it on the mountain)

Cavalleria Rusticana

when you left out for New York City
I dreamt the opera house burnt down firemen
brayed baritone and tenor
divas keened to their blazing wardrobes
and when sun rose on smoking ruin
there stood the warped black seatless wire chairs
late of the merry Cafe Momus
there were Carmen's crickly castanets

and treading Traviata's crystal
and Pagliacci's big bass charcoal drum
I relived your fond Greyhound farewell
bus stairwell filled with your aria
mine from atop the lumpy mailbags
rose above the resonant gateways
and when I touched at the aftermath
each warm black note sang itself again

A Poet's Fate

caught up in a whirlwind
up into the third heaven
my little kettlebottom head
so coarse a grain of destiny
slang truth cussword coarse
      RICH MEN STEAL YOU BLIND

yes and when the deathbed hand
of that cunning old pilgrim
who was my great grandfather
felt of the candor bump
on my unborn undead noggin
laid upon me his biblical blessing
brighter than snow on wool
      RICH MEN STEAL YOU BLIND

yes and when Pap Cunningham
passed on to me his zzbop zzbopski
me his favorite daughter's
me his favorite granddaughter's
me his favorite great granddaughter's
wild child little baby boy
A KALLY MOE SHONDO
watch your windworn step child
one tornado to the tother
      RICH MEN STEAL YOU BLIND

Bugville Kaballah

Bees of mine do what they desire in the hive-
deeds of absolute yet small dimensions,
Buddha-winters, Buddha-summers, to the sweet
        lion-colored combs.

Ants of mine always make me their emperor,
who brings reforms, grafts to their bug-believings
free and sundry forms of the Original Face
        with kingly feelers.

But my silverfish—my yes, my silverfish-
cling nervously to their paradise pages,
for all letters were scattered to begin with
        and still one's missing.

Honky Tonk Marot

In the good old days, hang what now appears
Lovers were so anxious of the name
Promises were promises no matter what came
And romance went oh twenty thirty years.

But now sing lucky if it last three beers—
Why, they'd call that a low down shame
                    In the good old days.

Listen: till some new news reaches my ears
To make the past and present the same
Here where things are so muddy and so tame
I'll run love's stream back to where it clears
                    In the good old days.

The Night Watch

above it all I'm the satellite watching
lonesome cities lighting the Trans-Siberian Railway clusters
of burnpipes on the Persian Gulf
here they come   there they go
squidlights flooding the Sea of Japan

and even though I'm a speechless object
shoot fire I keep an eye on the whole planet
I spy out David Boothe—hey, Boothe! you down there
 in your bachelor trailer on Fenwick Mountain
between the dazzle of the Eastern Seaboard and the bright
   Midwest—
hey Boothe, straighten up! there's a blue baby mouse
   in that pile of dishes!

and I am ever so concerned about the Enlightened
   Democracies
and Celebes and the lightline of the Nile
(hey! is that Mozart's face aglow in Central Europe?)
the flames across the African grasslands
Amazonia dotted with slash and burn
and the campfire that Boothe and Billy have scattered
a coal shining here   another over there
what a spark-eyed sight to see

SELECTED POEMS

Linoleum: Camoflage of the Absolute

I found your name written in an old hymn book:
some heathen called you "Hot Pants"
right above "The trumpets are a-sounding"

well you won't last long respectable
that's one thing I'll say by God
for I know how you are

you're like the flowers on linoleum
God-awful to have in the church house
But T-total-perfect for all night dancin

Finishing Touches

For the first time in my life
I awoke completely honest
getting up off your linoleum
from amid the packed boxes
in the middle of your last night
telling you I really love you I really love you
and you too skeptical sleepy really to understand
mumbling mnfh yeah
why
that was the final moment
the last straw of perfect romance
of the Baal of arguments and deceptions
of the living hilljack Jerusalem
where my final satisfying dream slumber
became true love burnt down to glowing alligator rafters

Hillbilly Toscanini

when first I contracted the Barbry Allen fever
I was standing on a brick sidewalk
in front of a brick drugstore in Pennsboro
and here you come

all the bricks commenced to floating around
the MacBricky was how you say vouty vouty
and I saw my courtship sail into action
in your throwaway smile

not but one medicine they had for it then
scads and scads of Pall Malls Pell Mells
and you said how do you feel PaPa
you both doctor and germ

wellsir I never enjoyed a disease so much
ooch ouch I moaned ooch ouch
a sinking feeling no a rising no a sinking
BRICK TRAMPOLINE!

that's what drove me out the next Friday
staggering from the hoohaw sidelines
to conduct the Saint Marys High School Band
a hillbilly Toscanini

No Regrets

your good looks
were the brownest words in the almanac
the fifth largest planet
the new element and the world series

your face was naïve
like a chronicle caught in a lie
a fox in a garden
not knowing how good looking how naïve how naïve;

I was an animal out of a book
and you were pure progress
but steps had been taken
assumptions had been made

you hurried me off
when we quit seeing one another
sweeping the sidewalk the cut grass
sorry saying sorry sweeping sorry goodbye

Guard Duty

I wake up in the night in the hills of West Virginia
in the house of my eighty-four-year-old cousin
a single star in his bathroom window
and old white doorcurtain window with tree in fog behind
takes me back to you
                         love old snake
here comes the aw shit love feeling

I run my hand over the tufted bedquilt
trying to recall my dream of raccoon-faced leaves
                         dawn's arriving
I will fill one of your old stockings
with Blue Dragon Sevin Dust
and sprinkle for the bugs
I will pick the wax beans
thinking of the old folks fingers
I touched in their coffins

The Refounding of Saint Marys

despite the undeniable fact
that I was fluent
in the Chicken Track Language
of the Ancient Mound Builders
of old West Virginia

despite Alexander Creel
on a midnight paddlewheel
horsethief asleep
on the starlit steamboat
on the cold muddy Ohio

you called me "a living enigma"
I called you "a female Jack Dempsey"
I was Luis Firpo
ah Wild Bull of the Pampas
the title was in your grasp

but now the gangster weeps
at the Hawaiian music
and a tear drop glistens
on the key of the grand piano
in the four o'clock night club

and a tear drop falls upon the Bible
and magnifies the Word
the sad smiling Virgin appears now
on the West Virginia shore
as I float now to Mardi Gras

Payne's Place

of all them fifty thousand-odd kisses
there was one in particular
in your old black Chevy
outside Payne's beer joint
when we fired up a reefer
sat goofed on love
when suddenly
with your cool snapbean fingers
you pressed into my lips
that cracked half a benny
and all at once laid the kissereenymoe
on your wide-eyed Christ of the cornfields

thens when I forgot
everything I learned at the High Hat
thens when I forgot
all I knew from the Hill Top
baby
you have no idea

The Country Jakes

Speaking merely as one wolf in a zoot suit
Among many wolves in zoot suits
I say to you in the Wake Island bebop language
SEND MORE EVIL
Twirling my big long watch chain round and round
And I say:

The country jakes of old
Subtle sullen awesome acute
Were far too profound for the 19th century
What a mellow bunch

Like a clanky water dipper
          How awkward!
Like a pack of Sen-Sen
          How lasting!
Like ice just beginning to melt
          How self-effacing!
Like a hollow in the spring
          How refreshing!
Like walking across a mop job
          How polite!
Like a swinging bridge
          How surprising!

Who, full of shit, is pure?
Who sits under a shade tree
And brings about the harvest!

O them old time hillbillies
Slip through your fingers like nothing...

Aiee

my discoveries are all so invisible
I wonder if my descendants will go about
knocking their knuckles on the daisies unthinking:
I sure felt it a lucky privilege
to sit there on your fleurdelis sofa
why it was like crossing a mop job
or a hundred free lessons with Madame Lazonga
a privilege to see the dubieties in your eyes
as we threw our duds on the linoleum
a privilege an irritating privilege:
asleep in Jesus blessed sleep
from which none ever wakes to weep
in undisturbed and calm repose
unorchen by the something something moss
my Argyll socks all turned to horseweed
a groundhog hole in my side
the sun shining so beautiful

THE SOUPBEAN POETS

The Soupbean Poets, 1977, Antioch Book Store, Beckley, West Virginia
Front Row: Bob Snyder, P.J. Laska
Back Row: Bob Henry Baber, David Chafins, Pauletta Hansel, Gail Amburgey
Photo by Bill Blizzard

THE SOUPBEAN POETS

The Soupbean Poets—named by Pauletta Hansel—are a bunch of mountain writers who became friends at Antioch College/Appalachia during the mid-1970s in Beckley, West Virginia. Such keen interaction of lives and styles is not usual in the quest for lyric voice, and if the rest isn't history, it sure is fun.

My explanation of Soupbeanism begins with its nonchalance about the near and far reach of urban modernism, including post-modernism (compare Eliot's *Wasteland* with Tone Loc's "Wild Thing"). Take the start of this famous but toplofty poem:

> *I sit in one of the dives*
> *On Fifty-second Street*

A poor choice of place. If Auden had seen fit to hold on to his seat, he might have seen Nat Cole, Lady Day, Art Tatum, or Yardbird. This artist and his heirs—less talented, for sure—are out of touch with pretty much all that makes life interesting or contentious, comic or tragic. The alleged breakdown of a central standard in American poetry is just the local recognition of the central fact.

We've been clear on this where other Appalachian poets—opting for Modernism Lite or something even worse, like Jesse Stuart—have not. Our clarity has been scouted [sic] as brash, as have our uncompromised political views. As Cratis Williams knew, the Local Color movement has more lives than Dracula. But genteel complaints about stereotypes and defensive junk pasted over with regional markers are downright sleazy when the industrialists and politicians are stealing Christ off the cross and coming back for the nails.

It's funny we've been jumped on for being ideological, because that's what we see as the dead base in national and regional styles—ideological mannerism. Mountain people have a way of knowing themselves, but it doesn't lie in that direction. Perfect conviction ignores itself. Little absolutes like ours clear a way for the transparent pursuit of human and artistic ends, free of artiness and of ethnic posturing. What I now see about our poetry which was hidden or implicit when we began is the passionate, basic, and free way of exploring thought and feeling. The stylistic affinities begin there, with that full throttle.

But rather than preach I should urge the reader to look into our corner of the human barnyard for what it's worth. I believe that bohemian roots take strongly to good provincial soil: *at dolor in lacrimas verterat omne merum* ("Till sorrow turns all the wine to tears." Tibullus, I: v:38).

—*Bob Snyder*

From *The Sow's Ear: Poetry Review*, Winter, Vol.11, No. 1, 1990, p.6.

About the Author

Bob Snyder reading at Lees Junior College, 1977
Photo by Pauletta Hansel

BOB SNYDER (1937-1995) was from St. Marys, West Virginia. He was the son of Robert W. and Malwina Snyder, and a graduate of St. Marys High School. A well known poet and literary critic, he was the author of *We'll See Who's a Peasant* (1977). He was an Editor of *Soupbean Anthology* (1977) and the periodical *What's a Nice Hillbilly Like You...?* He graduated from West Virginia University with a B.A., the University of Cincinnati with an M.A. and from Harvard University with an Ed.D. He taught at Lesley College in Cambridge, MA and from 1972 to 1978 he was the Director of Antioch College/Appalachia in Beckley, WV.

Jimmie's, Beckley, WV 2020.
Photo by Stephanie Ketz